QUICK PRAYERS

FOR THE
MIND, SOUL
AND
SPIRIT

BELINDA HAYDEN

Published, printed, and distributed in the United States by Belinda Hayden, Fort Meyers, Florida.

The author of this book does not dispense spiritual advice or prescribe any technique as a form of treatment for physical, emotional, or medical problems without the advice of a physician, either directly or indirectly. The author intends to offer information of a general nature to help you in your quest for emotional and spiritual well-being. In the event you use any of the information in this book for yourself, which is your constitutional right, the author or publisher assume no responsibility for your actions.

Cover Design – Okomota
Editing and Layout – The Self-Publishing Maven
Interior Design – Istvan Szabo, Ifj., Sapphire Guardian International

ISBN: 978-0-578-67837-5

Thank you, Bishop Dr. Eric Johnson and First Lady Dr. Denise Johnson, for giving birth to a praying ministry. I did not know how to pray before submitting under your leadership. You taught me how to seek God through his word, to build a personal relationship and to develop a fervent effective prayer life. I am forever grateful for all that you've imparted into my life.

Thank you, Robin Devonish, for entering my life at just the right time and inspiring me to go above and beyond what I can see myself doing.

I dedicate this book to my husband, Robert Hayden
and children (Kanisha Brown, Freddie Brown,
Mia Hayden, Ronnetra Hayden).
Every time I think of you, it becomes fuel to my
prayer life and walk with God.
I Love You!

Why was this book created?

When life happens, there are times where we need to get a quick prayer in to embrace peace and to soothe our body, mind and soul. Of course, one should have prayer time and devotion where considerable time is spent with God, however, a fast 'Lord Help' never hurt anyone.

This book was created as a tool for you to pray for a subject or need you have in a quick moment. Filled with declaration of scripture, all prayers are consistent with one having a repentant heart and receiving God's forgiveness and mercy.

Keep this tool in near for encouragement and in times where you can't find the words to say in that moment. My prayer is that this book and Holy Spirit will help your mind, soul, and spirit in Jesus name. Amen!

CONTENTS

MIND

Jesus said to him, "You shall love the Lord your God with all your heart, with all your soul, and with all your mind." – Matthew 22:37

IF CONFUSED...

Dear Heavenly Father, I come to you in the name of Jesus and repent of all my sins. Cleanse and wash me in the blood of Jesus. Lord, today I release all confusion out of my life and cast down every imagination and high thought that exalts itself against the knowledge of God. I bring all into captivity and every thought to the obedience of Christ.

I trust in you Lord with all my heart and I won't lean to my own understanding. Your word says that a doubled minded person is unstable in all his ways. I will not waver in my mind but claim stability. Lord, please send my helper the Holy Spirit to bring all things into my remembrance. Let your peace saturate my mind. Let me not forget your promises for my life. Let my praise forever confuse to enemy, in Jesus name, Amen.

IF FEARFUL...

Dear Heavenly Father, I come to you in the name of Jesus and repent of all my sins. Wash and cleanse me in the blood of Jesus. I release all my fears of failure, rejection, death and any other fears that desires to control my life. I have walked in and been paralyzed in fear long enough.

God, I've missed many opened doors and opportunities that you've prepared for me because of fear. Lord, I wasn't created to have a spirit of fear, but was created with love, power and a sound mind.

Now is the time to take my life back by faith. For without Faith it's impossible to please you. I want to live a life that is pleasing to you. I shall walk in boldness. I am more than a conqueror. I can do all things through Christ Jesus who strengthens me. I'm no longer fearful, but I am confident in who you've created me to be. I am strong and courageous. What A mighty God I serve. The one who fights for me. So, I will not be afraid because you are with me. Your rod and your staff comfort me. You prepared a table before me in the presents of my enemies. Today I walk in victory. Lord, I thank you for breaking fear off me, in Jesus name, Amen.

IF ANXIOUS...

Dear Heavenly Father, I come to you in the name of Jesus. I repent of all my sins. Cleanse and wash me in the blood of Jesus. Lord I need your protection because I am facing Anxiety. I don't want to feel this way anymore. I will not allow worry to consume my mind because I know that you have everything under your control. Help me to cast all my cares on you. When my heart is overwhelmed and beating fast, I bind palpitations and thoughts of having a heart attack. I bind the spirit of death from my mind. Help me to meditate on your word. Give me peace as I keep my mind stayed on you. I trust you with my life. I know you are the lamp under my feet, the light to my path and you will lead me in the right direction as I acknowledge you in all my ways. Thank you for total freedom, in Jesus name, Amen.

IF WORRIED...

Dear Heavenly Father, I come to you in the name of Jesus. I repent of all my sins. Cleanse and wash me in the blood of Jesus. Lord I release all my worries to you; for I know that you care for me. Your word says that you clothe the lilies of the field and the birds of the air, so what is my situation to you? I know that you will come through right on time.

I will not allow negative thoughts to control my mind. I will not be anxious concerning any situation or about my life. I know that your yoke is easy, and your burden is light. Today I find my rest in you. I receive your peace that surpasses all understanding. Thank you for always being there for me, in Jesus name, Amen.

IF STRESSED...

Dear Heavenly Father, I come to you in the name of Jesus. I repent of all my sins. Cleanse me and wash me in the blood of Jesus. Purify my heart and mind so my thoughts are pure, holy and righteous. Today, I release stress to you and come out of agreement with it. No longer will stress control my life and cause me to isolate myself from those who love me. No longer will stress control my mind and cause me to feel like I will live the rest of my life this way. Today I'm breaking free from this mental torment, for by the stripes of Jesus I am healed.

I am a child of God and I know that if I cry out to you for help, you will hear me and deliver me from all my troubles. I know that you will never leave nor forsake me, so I will wait patiently for you to send me your peace. I know that you are fighting this battle for me and that victory is mine today through the power of the blood of Jesus. When feeling stressed I will trust you and meditate on your word day and night until I get a breakthrough. Through my faith and your word, I am healed from the stressors of life. I will live my life stress free and will no longer cripple myself or accept what the enemy is throwing my way emotionally. Thank you for relieving my stress and for being a mind regulator. Lead and guide me by your Holy Spirit today, in Jesus name, Amen.

IF HAVING SUICIDAL THOUGHTS...

Dear Heavenly Father, I come to you in name of Jesus repenting of all my sins. Wash and cleanse me in the Blood of Jesus. Lord I am battling with suicidal thoughts. I feel unworthy and like no one cares about me. At times, I see no point in living, but deep down inside I want to live. I'm tired of feeling this way. God, please rescue me from this torment. Save me from myself and from the enemy that is trying to kill, steal and destroy me. Renew within me a new heart and a right spirit.

Lord, I know you have wonderful plans for me which include hope and a future. I believe you created me for a purpose. I need your help to find it. Your spirit within me is greater than suicidal thoughts. I receive your power and word to fight back and plead the blood of Jesus over my mind and emotions. No weapon formed against me will prosper.

I cancel every lie the enemy whispered in my ear and take authority over this great life you have given me. I will fulfill the purpose for which I was born. This is a new day and beginning. I thank you for the unconditional love you have for me, in Jesus name, Amen.

IF COMPARING YOURSELF TO OTHERS...

Dear Heavenly Father I come to you in the name of Jesus. I repent of all my sins. Cleanse and wash me in the blood of Jesus. Lord, I will no longer compare myself to others. I will keep my eyes on you the author and finisher of my faith. I declare that I'm not conformed to this world but transformed by the renewing of my mind. I will not be led by jealousy and selfish ambition.

I will not be controlled by envy. Lord, I commit my ways to you, and I trust you with my life. Thank you for being my shepherd I have all I need in you, in Jesus name, Amen.

IF YOU WANT WISDOM...

Dear Heavenly Father I come to you in the name of Jesus. I repent of all my sins. Cleanse and wash me in the blood of Jesus. Lord I am asking for your wisdom to increase in my life. You are the one that gives wisdom and from your mouth comes knowledge and understanding. Help me to be wise in my living and attentive to your word in the way that I should live.

You say if anyone lacks wisdom they should ask. Today, I'm asking, knocking and seeking and I believe the doors of wisdom will be opened to me. I will gain a heart of wisdom. Thank you Lord giving me what I need to make the right decisions in life, in Jesus name, Amen.

IF YOU WANT HEALING...

Dear Heavenly Father I come to you in the name of Jesus. I repent of all my sins. Cleanse and wash me in the blood of Jesus. Lord, I surrender to your healing power over my body and believe your stripes I am healed. I believe your word and that you are a miracle worker. I know that your grace is made perfect in my weakness. I know you will comfort me in my suffering. I will not allow fear to control me for you will restore my health and heal my wounds. You will save me from all my distress. Despite the doctors report I know that you are in control and I believe your report concerning my health, in Jesus name, Amen.

SOUL

"For what profit is it to a man if he gains the whole world, and loses his own soul? Or what will a man give in exchange for his soul?" – Matthew 16:26

FOR SALVATION...

Dear Heavenly Father I come to you in the name of Jesus. I repent of all my sins. Cleanse and wash me in the blood of Jesus. Lord I admit that I am a sinner and ask you to come into my heart and save me. I confess with my mouth and I believe in my heart that you are my Lord and Savior. Thank you for dying on the cross for me. Help me to live in a way that is well pleasing. Fill me with the *power* of your Holy Spirit and teach me your ways. Lord, show me your will for my life through your word and break every curse off my life that will hold me back. Help me to walk away from everyone who means me no good so that I can grow in my salvation, in Jesus name, Amen.

GIVING THANKS AND PRAISE...

Dear Heavenly Father I come to you in the name of Jesus. I repent of all my sins. Cleanse and wash me in the blood of Jesus. Lord today I lift thanks and praise to you. Your word says let everything that has breathe praise the Lord. I give thanks to you with my whole heart and will glorify your name forever. Praises will continually flow from my mouth. I won't let my trails get the best of me because I know all things are working together for my good. Let my praise confuse the enemy. Let my praise cause him to stop in his tracks. Let my praise fight my battle for me, in Jesus name, Amen.

TO WORSHIP...

Dear Heavenly Father I come to you in the name of Jesus. I repent of all my sins. Cleanse and wash me in the blood of Jesus. Lord, show me how to worship you in all areas of my life. Your word says that those that worship you must do so in spirit and in truth. Help me to discipline myself to sit quietly in your presence without distraction and worship you with everything within me. I lift my hands to you, surrendered in the splendor of your holiness. Let your presence fill me up until it overflows, in Jesus name, Amen.

FOR LOVE...

Dear Heavenly Father I come to you in the name of Jesus. I repent of all my sins. Cleanse and wash me in the blood of Jesus. Lord, please release an overflow of your love into my life. Your word says love covers a multitude of sins and rules in all things. Fill me with your love that forgives those who've offended me. Help me to love without hesitating. I invite your love to cast out all hate and fears in my life. Help me to love my enemies and without limits and so people will see your presences and know that I am your disciple and they will draw to your presence. Thank you so much for loving me with everlasting unconditional love, in Jesus name, Amen.

HOLDING UNFORGIVENESS...

Dear Heavenly Father. I repent of all my sins.
Cleanse me and wash me in the blood of Jesus. Lord
I come to you in humility and confession of holding
unforgiveness in my heart. I don't want to live my
life like this. I know I'm wrong for holding on to the
hurt but help me to release it. Help me to forgive
for I understand that if I don't forgive others then
my heavenly father cannot forgive me. Lord I need
your forgiveness every day and today I let it all go. I
lay every offense, negative word and what
happened on the cross.

I receive forgiveness in my heart and your
unconditional love to move forward. I will not walk
around with bitterness and hatred in my heart.
Thank you for walking me through this difficult
process. Thank you for freedom and a new
beginning in you, in Jesus name, Amen.

HOLDING ANGER...

Dear Heavenly Father I come to you in the name of Jesus. I repent of all my sins. Cleanse and wash me in the blood of Jesus. Lord, today I release all anger to you. I do not want the sun to go down on my wrath or anger and cause me to sin. I don't want to make a foolish decision because of my temper. Help me not to shout or yell but let me respond with a soft answer and in a way I won't regret. I want my words to be pleasing to you.

Lord, help me to be quick to listen, slow to speak, and slow to anger so I can continue to walk in the righteousness you desire. Let your love fill me up because love is not easily angered. Thank you Lord for bringing healing into my life, in Jesus name, Amen.

HOLDING HATRED...

Dear Heavenly Father I come to you in the name of Jesus. I repent of all my sins. Cleanse and wash me in the blood of Jesus. Lord, today I ask to be cleansed of any hatred in my heart. I forgive those who did me wrong and don't want to repay evil for evil. I want the love of God to shine on my life. Let your love drive out the all hate, bitterness, rage and anger I may hold. Your *love* covers all wrongs. I don't want to claim loving a God I don't see and hate a sister and brother that I do see. I will *love* my enemies and do good to those who hate me. I will walk in the way of righteousness all the days of my life. I want you to be pleased with my heart. Thank you for your word that always brings me back to a place of healing and deliverance, in Jesus name, Amen.

WALKING IN REBELLION...

Dear Heavenly Father I come to you in the name of Jesus. I repent of all my sins. Cleanse and wash me in the blood of Jesus. Lord I come out of agreement with rebellion. God, by your power and spirit I take authority over anything in my bloodline that would cause me to rebel against anything you've placed in my life. Father uproot it now by the power and blood of Jesus.

If I have any wounds of the past that was afflicted on me from any type of leadership help me to heal from them. I release every offense that causes me to struggle in this area. When I hear your voice, soften my hardened heart and lead me to repentance. I want to humble myself, submit to you Lord and not be devoured by my trials in life due to rebellion. I want to please you and hear you say well done good and faithful servant. Thank you for delivering me, in Jesus name, Amen.

WALKING IN PRIDE...

Dear Heavenly Father I come to you in the name of Jesus. I repent of all my sins. Cleanse and wash me in the blood of Jesus. Lord, today I cast out all pride in my life. I understand that pride comes before destruction and a haughty spirit before the fall.

Search me Lord, for you know my heart. I confess that I don't know it all. I don't want the enemy to devour me. I want to walk humbly before you; teach me to walk in your ways to be perfected for purpose. I cast down any selfish ambition or vain conceit within my heart. Thank you for uprooting any wicked ways within me, in Jesus name, Amen

FOR GOD'S STRENGTH...

Dear Heavenly Father I come to you in the name of Jesus. I repent of all my sins. Cleanse and wash me in the blood of Jesus. Lord you are my strength, strong tower and help when I'm in trouble. When I am weak, you are strong within me. I declare your word and believe I can do all things through Christ Jesus who strengthens me. Your word says if I wait on you, my strength will be renewed. I will wait on you with hope and praise in my heart.

God, thank you for being my rock, my fortress, and my deliverer; I take refuge in you. I will not walk in fear. I will be strong and courageous by your power that is within me, in Jesus name, Amen.

FOR BACKSLIDING...

Dear Heavenly Father I come to you in the name of Jesus. I repent of all my sins. Cleanse and wash me in the blood of Jesus. Lord I turn my life back to you. You've been so amazing to me and I allowed the enemy to deceive me and go back to my old ways.

I repent for backsliding and rebelling against you. Forgive me for leaving my first love, which is you. Lord renew my mind through your word. Restore everything I've allow the enemy to kill, steal and destroy. I will not hold on to guilt, shame or condemnation because I know that you are a forgiving God and you welcome me back with open arms. I humbly submit, turn away from those things that are not well pleasing and move forward with my new life with you, in Jesus name, Amen.

DELIVERANCE FROM FORNICATION...

Dear Heavenly Father I come to you in the name of Jesus. I repent of all my sins. Cleanse and wash me in the blood of Jesus. Lord, today I turn my life away from fornicating. I come out of agreement with all sexual sin against my body. I believe I am a temple of your Holy Spirit. I desire to live *holy* and *righteous* before you. Please help as I submit myself to you and resist the enemy.

I ask for strength as I sit in your presence in preparation for the person you want me to marry. Search my heart and take out all lust and perversion by the power of the blood of Jesus. Deliver me from any emotional, mental, or physical soul ties in the name of Jesus. Further I pray for your shield of protection. I close every door and promise to walk obediently in every area of my life, in the mighty name of Jesus, Amen.

FOR COMMITTING ADULTERY...

Dear Heavenly Father I come to you in the name of Jesus. I repent of all my sins. Cleanse and wash me in the blood of Jesus. Lord today I repent for opening the door of adultery. My marriage should be honored, and bed kept pure. Father I cannot ignore this area of my life any longer. Though my spouse may not see me, you do. Give me godly sorrow that works repentance in my life. It is your will for me to be sanctified. I don't want to destroy myself of my family. Search my heart and uproot all lust. Fill me with your holiness and righteousness. Let today be a new beginning, in Jesus name, Amen.

SPIRIT

"For as the body without the spirit is dead, so faith without works is dead also." – James 2:26

GOOD HEALTH...

Dear Heavenly Father I come to you in the name of Jesus. I repent of all my sins. Cleanse and wash me in the blood of Jesus. Lord, I ask for restored health. I know that you want me to be in perfect health even as my soul prospers.

I desire to be healthy spiritually, mentally, emotionally and physically so that I may do your will. I know there is a great calling on my life since I was in my mother's womb. By your strength, I break every eating habit that harms my body. I embrace the will power to eat the right foods, and the discipline to exercise daily. My body belongs to you, as I am a temple of the Holy Spirit. I want to live a long healthy life for your glory, in Jesus name, Amen.

GREAT FAITH...

Dear Heavenly Father I come to you in the name of Jesus. I repent of all my sins. Cleanse and wash me in the blood of Jesus. Lord, today I receive faith that moves mountains. Your word says, faith comes by hearing and by hearing the word of God. Lord, reveal those faith scriptures for daily devotion and to grow my faith. Your word says, now faith is the substance of things hoped for and the evidence of things that are not seen. Though I don't see things with my natural eyes, my faith will know that you are working things out for my good. I will not lose heart nor walk in fear because you are with me. Thank you for never leaving me, in Jesus name, Amen.

ASKING FOR HUMILITY...

Dear Heavenly Father I come to you in the name of Jesus. I repent of all my sins. Cleanse and wash me in the blood of Jesus. Lord, I come to you asking for a spirit of humility. Help me to understand your word that says, 'if your people who are called by your name would humble themselves and pray and seek your face and turn from every wicked way then you will hear from heaven and heal our land.'

Today, as I turn to you in prayer, committing my ways and heart asking you heal me from all manner of pride. Lord I don't want to fall or go down the road of destruction. Therefore, I submit my life to you. Clothe me with compassion, kindness, humility, gentleness and patience, in Jesus name, Amen.

HEALING FROM REJECTION...

Dear Heavenly Father I come to you in the name of Jesus. I repent of my sins and ask that you wash me in the blood of Jesus. Today, I cast all rejection out of my life by the power and blood of Jesus. Lord, I seek you to learn more about me. Help me to see myself through your eyes. God, I know you accept me for I am fearfully and wonderfully made by you. I am unique and there's no other person like me and my identity is in you. Though others may reject me, you will never leave nor forsake me. I embrace your holy spirit, healing and love from any feelings I felt when rejected.

I will no longer draw back into a shell when others fail to see the best in me. I will no longer condemn myself and feel like a failure when rejected. I declare that I will continue to blossom like a beautiful butterfly, in Jesus name, Amen.

RELEASE FROM GUILT...

Dear Heavenly Father. I come to you in the name of Jesus. I repent of all my sins and ask you to wash me in the blood of Jesus. Purify my heart and keep my mind. I embrace thoughts that are pure, holy and righteous. I confess that I am in a battle with the spirit of guilt. Today, I release those feelings to you and resist the spirit taking over my life. No longer will I let guilt control my life and cause me to isolate from those who love me. No longer will guilt control my mind, arrest my spirit or life.

Today I break free from the mental torment that guilt carries, declaring, that by the stripes of Jesus I am healed. I am a child of God. I know if I cry out to you for help, you will hear me and deliver me from my troubles. I receive your peace and know you are fighting this battle for me. Victory is mine today by the power and blood of Jesus.

Thank you for your word that I can meditate on day and night for transformation. Through my faith and your word, I am healed. Thank you for lifting me out of this dark place. Thank you for being a mind regulator. Lead and guide me by your Holy Spirit today, in Jesus name, Amen.

RELEASE FROM CONDEMNATION...

Dear Heavenly Father I come to you in the name of Jesus. I repent of all my sins. Cleanse and wash me in the blood of Jesus. Lord, I release all condemnation to you and embrace your words which says, 'there is no condemnation to those who are in Christ Jesus.'

Lord, search my heart and thoughts; renew my heart with a right spirit. God, you are greater than condemnation! Today I will walk in the newness you've prepared for me. I will not look back to my past, but I will walk boldly into my wonderful future. Thank you Lord for leaving your word which has brought me freedom, in Jesus name, Amen.

RELEASE FROM HOPELESSNESS…

Dear Heavenly Father I come to you in the name of Jesus. I repent of all my sins. Cleanse and wash me in the blood of Jesus. Lord, I release all feelings of hopelessness to you. Your word says, 'hope deferred makes the heart sick.' I admit that I have allowed life's frustrations and discouragement to cause my heart to become sick; therefore, I have lost hope.

Today I declare that my hope is restored because of your vehicle called faith. I am motivated to take the necessary steps toward change. I believe that there is a future for me and for those connected to me and decree my hope will not be cut off because it's in you, in Jesus name, Amen.

OVERFLOW

*"The threshing floors shall be full of wheat,
And the vats shall overflow with new wine and oil."*
– Joel 2:24

PRAYER FOR MY FINANCES...

Dear Heavenly Father I come to you in the name of Jesus. I repent of all my sins. Cleanse and wash me in the blood of Jesus. Lord, I lift my finances up to you believing you will supply all my needs according to your riches and glory. I break the spirit of poverty, financial curses and lack in Jesus name. Help me to be a faithful tithe giver. I declare that I am not a lover of money and greed but am a good steward who will use the supply for what it's intended. Lord, stretch what you provide so that I may be available to work for you and not for money.

God, I trust you in this area of my life. I will seek the kingdom of God and everything else will be added. I understand that as my soul prospers so will I as you have given me the power to get wealth. Lord, show me how to utilize every idea and creativity that you have given me to bring in finances to sustain my family. Again, I declare that I am a good steward who maintains a budget. Lead me by your Holy Spirit with wisdom and clarity of mind. Thank you, Lord, for always making ways out of no way, in Jesus name, Amen.

PRAYER FOR MY SPOUSE...

Dear Heavenly Father I come to you in the name of Jesus. I repent of all my sins. Cleanse and wash me in the blood of Jesus. Lord, I lift my spouse to you. I thank you for the one you have given me for better or worse, through sickness and health. As we walk together as one, be with us to stand together in unity and sanctification. I bind any division, communication barriers and declare we are a three-strand cord not easily broken. We are not enemies, but a couple who will walk together and always pray in the name of Jesus.

May your unconditional love flood our souls; teach us the love you desire for us to have for each other. I desire to have the type of love that... covers sins, is patient, is kind, and not envious. I don't want to have love that boasts, is proud, dishonorable, self-seeking or angry. I pray for a love that endures all things and doesn't keep track of wrongs. I decree a healthy marriage filled with love, in Jesus name, Amen.

PRAYER FOR MY CHILDREN...

Dear Heavenly Father I come to you in the name of Jesus. I repent of all my sins. Cleanse and wash me in the blood of Jesus. Lord today I stand in the gap for my children. I repent for anytime I haven't been the parent you called me to be. Father, I pray your shield of protection around them. I break any generational curses off their life by the power and blood of Jesus.

Lord, guide my children in the way they should go. Give me parent wisdom to raise them so they will never depart from your presence. Father, please give me the strength to be a supportive parent in whatever life throws at them. I ask you help me to love them unconditionally, casting out all fear, and the ability to look past their sins.

I declare by your power and spirit that no weapon formed against them will prosper. Release your warring angels to fight on their behalf. My children will and are great in you. Thank you for my children for they are a blessing to me, in Jesus name, Amen.

PRAYER FOR MY EXTENDED FAMILY...

Dear Heavenly Father I come to you in the name of Jesus. I repent of all my sins. Cleanse and wash me in the blood of Jesus. Lord, today I lift my extended family to you. I ask that your Holy Spirit breathe life upon us. I break every generational curse to the third and fourth generation by the powerful blood of Jesus. Let there be no division, for your word says a house divided cannot stand and this word is true for family. Help us to stand strong as a fortified wall. Show my family how to display love to and for one another. Help us to create a stronger bond, walk without offense and the guide us on how to settle any differences that will move us to forgiveness and reconciliation.

Father, please help us to be patient with one another. Give us the spiritual eyes to see that most of our battle is spiritual and the power to stand together and fight what may come to divide us,

Lord draw us closer to you and as a family so we will

know your perfect will for all our lives. I thank you for the miracles, breakthroughs, deliverance and healings I believe you will perform in my family, in Jesus name, Amen.